AF265158

IL GENERALE RAFAELE DE RIEGO.

ALL'ECCELLENTISSIMA SIGNORA,

GIOVANNA ELISABETTA,

CONTESSA DI OXFORD E MORTIMER.

Tu il cui pensier di libertà grandeggia,
Inclita donna, dell'uom forte accetta
L'efficie in don, che fè tremar la Reggia
Ei Tiranni congiunti a rea vendetta
E poicche il Tago di fellon spesseggia
Cadde, e gli empj saziò vittima eletta
Tu che di patrio amore in seno hai tanto
Il riguarda, e se puoi trattieni il pianto.

Price 3ˢ6ᵃ

Printed by C. Hullmandel.

London Dec. 1823. Pub.ᵈ by R. J. Partridge, 4 Royal Arcade, Pall Mall.

MEMOIRS

OF

THE LIFE

OF

DON RAFAEL DEL RIEGO.

BY A SPANISH OFFICER.

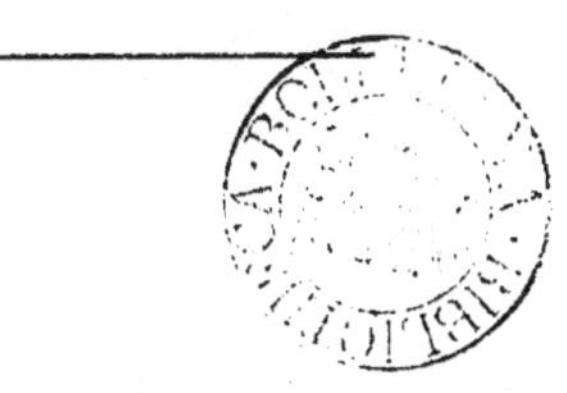

𝕷𝖔𝖓𝖉𝖔𝖓:

PRINTED FOR W. J. PARTRIDGE,

ROYAL ARCADE, PALL-MALL.

1823.

[Entered at Stationers' Hall.]

Printed by J. F. Dove, St. John's Square.

PREFACE.

In the following pages, we present to the English public, the life of one of those men of rare and extraordinary genius, that in the lapse of ages, rise above the political horizon, and seem destined to change the fate of nations.

The object of the publication is not to gratify idle curiosity ; nor do we limit ourselves to paying a well-merited tribute of eulogy to a man who is entitled to the gratitude of his countrymen, and the admiration of posterity. Our primary wish is to afford a useful lesson to every nation desirous of releasing itself from the galling yoke of arbitrary power, and to show how intricate and dangerous the career of revolution is, when undertaken without the cordial co-operation of all those whose welfare depends upon its success, to demonstrate the impossibility of retreating in that career, without touching the verge of a precipice at every step; in fact, to teach the uninformed, that the fortunate or unsuccessful issue of events, is connected with the fate of individuals who are instrumental in bringing them about; and that national ingratitude is a crime to which those, who render themselves guilty of it, become the wretched victims.

Let any one contemplate Spain in 1818, and Spain at this moment, comparing each with Constitutional Spain, and say how enormous must be the villany of men who have made the laws succumb to arbitrary authority, order to anarchy, intelligence to ignorance, the liberty of the press to the Inquisition, and common sense to fanaticism. It is one of the attributes of human nature to ameliorate its condition by all the means within its reach. Persecutions, fetters, scaffolds, will never repress this irresistible inclination; and wherever men blessed with the faculty of using their reasoning powers, exist, there will be found protectors for the oppressed, enemies to tyrants, and well-nerved arms to break disgraceful yokes, to burst the painful chain of thraldom.

This was the crime of General Riego; and it is one never pardoned by those who banquet upon a nation's blood, and derive enjoyment from the groans of victims, and the maledictions of slaves.

With a rapid pencil we have sketched a picture, that it is presumed will interest the sympathies of every man who has not renounced the honest feelings of his own dignity. A mere sketch is given, because minute details would only tone down, and enfeeble the strong touches of which the portrait of a man, that appeared but for a few instants on the political scene, is composed. Four or five remarkable events embrace his whole life; but even this limited number suffices to display transcendent qualities, great virtues, unsullied intentions, correct sentiments; and, above all, an admirable perseverance that falls to the lot of few, and which is so well entitled to unqualified praise, if directed to the accomplishment of a noble and generous action.

The life of Riego will probably be read in every civilized country, for the cause he defended is not that of a single nation, but of the whole world. Where the contest is between despotism and popular rights, there reigns a community of interests among all who dread the yoke of arbitrary power. There are but two grand divisions of men in modern society, the oppressors and the oppressed.

The facts herein given to the public, furnish many useful lessons, from which rulers may learn to moderate their desires, not to abuse the patience of the people; to respect their privileges, spare their blood, and pay deference to the imprescriptible rights of humanity. The people may learn gratitude towards those who protect them ; to distinguish those who are their real enemies; to answer the call of patriotism ; and what is more important still, to know how dangerous every capitulation with a despot is, and how inherent in their nature it is to avenge themselves upon those by whom they have been spared in the most critical moments.

LIFE OF RIEGO.

Don Rafael del Riego y Nuñez, was born in the year 1785, at Tuña, a little village of the district of Tineo, in the principality of Asturias. His parents were of noble extraction: his father, Don Eugenio Antonio Riego, was a man of very comprehensive genius, and endowed with such a talent and facility for poetical composition, that Ovid's expression,

" *Quod tentabam dicere versus erat,*"

might fairly be applied to him. Many of his works remain inedited, but several have been published, and they shew that his natural inclination for poetry was not inferior to the delicacy of his acquired taste. Being established at Oviedo, where for ten years he was Chief Administrator of the Posts, he gave his sons the general education which, at that time, the children of persons of his rank in Spain received. After their elementary studies, and that of the Latin language, they were instructed in some of those sciences, there distinguished by the title of *mayores*, or superior, but in reality rendered very trifling by the defective methods, and still worse books, employed in teaching them. Riego passed his early years in these pursuits, until he obtained his father's permission to enrol himself in the regiment of the King's body guards. To gratify his wishes on this point, recourse was had to the influence of his uncle, the ex-minister of marine, Valdes, of whom we shall have to speak hereafter. Riego was nominated a Garde du Corps, and his dexterity in horsemanship, combined with his knowledge of horses, soon enabled him to make a conspicuous figure in that station.

Shortly after this epoch, the French troops invaded the Spanish territory, at a period of profound peace, and while the two nations were united by the most friendly intercourse. Spain was then governed by Don Manuel de Godoy, Prince of Peace, reigning favourite of Charles IV. and his Queen Maria Louisa. The revolution which

burst forth at the royal residence of Aranjuez, on
the night between the 18th and 19th of March,
1808, terminated the sway, and almost boundless
authority, of that personage. Riego being on duty
with his corps on that memorable night, ardently
took a part in the general movement, having for its
object the deliverance of Spain from an intolerable
bondage; yet he was one of those who distinguished themselves by successful endeavours to
save the life of the fallen favourite. At this period,
Joachim Murat, Grand Duke of Berg, was appointed Regent of Spain, and Riego, with all the
other guards who were implicated in the revolt of
Aranjuez, was sent prisoner to the Escurial. The
patriotism of the Spaniards now developed itself;
Riego's native province caught the flame, and gave
vent to one general blaze of enthusiasm. Im-
pelled by an eager desire of contributing his efforts to those of his countrymen, he found means
to evade the vigilance of his gaolers, escaped from
the Escurial, and traversing the mountains of Guada-
rama, reached Segovia at a moment when the inhabitants, having received intelligence that a French

division of 1000 men was advancing to occupy the city, were flying to arms, and preparing for its defence, but with no other means than those which their patriotic spirit, and eagerness to preserve the national independence, could administer. Riego participated the universal zeal; but after having examined, in company of an artillery officer, the fortifications, which were found in a most deplorable state; and being convinced that there was no possibility of resisting troops, who had excited the admiration of Europe by their courage and discipline, he quitted the city, and continued his route towards the Asturias. In the course of this journey, he resided some time with a family to which he was related, and they strongly impressed upon his mind the risks he exposed himself to, by wearing his Garde du Corps uniform, in a province entirely open to the French troops; and in fact occupied, or traversed by them in every direction. Yielding to representations, so just and so considerate, he abandoned a costume he was proud of wearing, for a dress of skins, such as is usually worn by shepherds in that country, and so disguised, traversed part of the province without impediment, until he reached Villalpando, where he was arrested on suspicion, and lodged in the common prison. The report of this circumstance accidentally reached the ears of an ecclesiastic, who, knowing Riego's family, became surety for him; he thus regained his liberty, and continued his journey to Leon, where he arrived on the 12th of June, at night. In that city he met his brother, Don Miguel del Riego, Canon of the Cathedral of Oviedo, who had repaired thither to deliver some important documents from the junta of the Asturias to that of Leon; there also the two brothers had the satisfaction of meeting their uncle Valdes, who, by the course of political events, was constrained to withdraw from his residence at Burgos, because he had refused to go to Bayonne, whither he had been summoned to take a part in the grand drama of which that place was the theatre.

Riego being made acquainted, by his brother, with the state of public feeling which spread over the Asturias, hastened thither with all possible speed; and on arriving at Oviedo, he found the streets filled with patriotic bands, formed from all ranks of society. Arming *en masse* proceeded rapidly; the junta of the Asturias, of which his brother was a member, directed this important movement, and he received a commission as Captain in the regiment of Tineo, one of the twenty-four corps that were armed, equipped, and sent into active service by that province.

The French troops now began to feel the difficulties, as well as dangers, of the arduous enterprise into which the ambition of their Chief had forced them. The first heroic defence of Saragossa, the stubborn resistance at Valencia, the battle of Rio Seco, the total destruction of a French division at Baylen, had proved to the soldiers of Napoleon, that they were to expect many obstinate and bloody contests, before they would be able to subjugate the Peninsula.

The principality of the Asturias equipped a division of 8,000 men to reinforce the army of Galicia, commanded by General Blake, and destined to defend the passes of Biscay. The command of the Asturian division was bestowed on Don Vincente

Maria Azevedo (an intimate friend of the Canon Riego), who appointed Don Rafael his aid-de-camp. Azevedo being far advanced in years, and borne down by infirmities, travelled in a carriage, surrounded by the aids-de-camp, and escorted by a small guard. This troop was attacked by a very superior force of the enemy; and being put to flight, every one forsook the General, except Riego, who saved him by giving up his own horse, and remaining on foot, exposed to the most imminent dangers; he had the satisfaction of seeing his patron escape, but was himself taken prisoner, and sent into France. This honourable trait of self-devotedness, was worthy of that man, who, in the sequel, never hesitated in sacrificing his private interests to the good of his country; and who, in his political career, invariably deemed himself a victim devoted to the general welfare.

During his captivity in France, he applied his whole attention to take advantage of the resources which that country opened to him for cultivating his natural genius, enlarging his understanding, and, above all, in perfecting himself in the military

science, to which he had a decided partiality, as well
as the requisite capacity for acquiring it.   He gave
himself up entirely to pursuits of literature ; he
acquired the French language in its utmost purity ;
obtained a competent knowledge of the English,
and carefully studied modern tactics; he gained
correct views of the general course of politics, and
imbibed, from the writings of philosophic publicists,
those philanthropic and beneficent doctrines, that
are calculated to promote the happiness of nations,
by securing to them laws analogous to their neces-
sities, and by destroying the evils which corrupt
society, from permitting the ease, comforts and
conveniences of life, that all are entitled to, and
all have a right to enjoy, to centre within the small
circle of a limited number of ranks and families.
He soon made himself capable of comparing the
absurd institutions of his own country, with the
permanent laws of universal legislation, founded
on reason and justice.   Possibly his fervent and
generous spirit, bounding forward to the future,
figured out in perspective the happiness of Spain,
for which he afterward laboured with so much zeal

and solicitude. The gentleness of his character, the easiness of his manners, and his unassuming modesty, endeared him to his comrades, and procured him a great number of friends. The hospitable reception given to the Spanish prisoners by the people of France, excited in him a very high esteem for that nation, then under the brilliant and seductive despotism of Napoleon, but now sunk into a more disgraceful slavery.

Riego returned to Spain after the peace, and continued his military career, in which merit, as much as his connexions, obtained him promotion.

. When the ungrateful Ferdinand, that man whom modern civilization rejects as a monstrous anomaly in an enlightened age, destroyed the compact with his people, and re-established a despotism, as barbarous and as repugnant to common sense as ever was that of the horrible times of Philip the Second; Spain, the country which had so recently shewn itself to the admiring eyes of all the world, as an heroic nation, in which the love of liberty and independence seemed the only impetus that gave it energy ; the country which had indignantly spurned the yoke of disgrace, that debased every other nation of the Continent ; yes ! Spain itself crouched to an implacable tyrant, thirsting for the blood of his subjects, and submitted to a government of goading autocracy, supported by fanaticism, in which the only law and mode of administration depended upon the caprices of the despot, and the rapacity of his satellites. Men of enlightened minds, who had, under the ephemeral reign of the Constitution established by the Cortes, felt the benefits of a liberal regime, would not groan under the atrocities of a truly Ottoman sceptre, swayed by the imbecile hand of Ferdinand. The love of liberty had taken root in the breasts of the military ; and when the armed force of the tyrants of Europe was converted into the irresistible instruments of their despotic will, the Spanish army burned with desire to put an end to the innumerable evils which afflicted their country. Discontent, exasperation, and hatred of oppression, pervaded the soldiery : these feelings were augmented, incensed, in proportion as Ferdinand disgracefully abandoned himself to the gratification of his revenge, which appeared to be one of the salient points of his character. Generals who had distinguished themselves in the war for independence, and who, by heroic achievements, which posterity will cherish the remembrance of, had delivered the Monarch from fetters he had voluntarily bound himself in, were left in obscurity, or pined in exile. Mina, Lacy, Porlier, Ballesteros, the Empecinado, were treated as officers of a common description, and even as men dangerous to the community; at the same time that places, riches, and honours, were bestowed with the hand of a prodigal upon cowardly and ignorant generals (so miscalled), who kept aloof in the hour of danger, and only shewed themselves after the victory was won, to flatter the bad passions of their master, and stimulate him to persecution and vengeance. It soon became apparent that the almost universal irritation had reached a point whence it was necessary to shew itself, and assume an active character. Mina endeavoured to re-establish the Constitution, and make himself master of the fortress of Pamplona; but his plan being defeated, he was forced to seek an asylum in France. Porlier and Lacy followed his example, in enterprises pregnant with difficulties and dangers; and both fell by the stroke of the executioner, victims to their heroic efforts. The spirit of resistance, however, assumed a more imposing form, in proportion as its designs were frustrated: one unsuccessful attempt was succeeded by plans for another, with increased hopes of more fortunate results; and despotism, dazzled by the imaginary splendours of its triumph, furnished, by the inexpertness of design, and faulty arrangement of its own measures, the combustibles for a wide-spreading explosion, from which it could not escape unhurt.

During the Peninsular war, and after the result of that very war which had given birth to the spirit of liberty and independence among the Spaniards, many of the Spanish colonies were incited to shake off the dominion of the mother country, and proclaim constitutions suitable to their actual situations, sanctioned by representative bodies that were the depositaries of the rights of their respective nations. Men who cannot discover in these events

a blazing beacon to announce the general emancipation of all the American continent, must possess
very limited perceptions, or be strangely blinded by
prejudice.

The hatred of the Creoles towards the Spaniards,
the examples of the United States of North
America, the rigours of the climate, the irresistible force of events that demonstrates to every people
the period of its political existence, must altogether
have announced to the counsellors of Ferdinand,
that the loss of the Colonies was inevitable ; and
that a falling nation, treasureless, exhausted by long
efforts, and split into contending parties, cannot
hope to subdue a vigorous and wealthy people, with
the broad Atlantic between it and the assailants,
and invited to independence as powerfully by natural affection for it, as by interest. But reflec-
tions like these could effect no impression upon
the pride and cupidity of an ignorant and corrupt
court. Russia, whose imperial Autocrat had formed
a close alliance with Ferdinand, urged on the ruin-
ous project of fitting out expeditions ; and orders

were issued for sending the flower of the Spanish youth to the shores of the new world.

A numérous army was assembled in the environs of Cadiz; the important duties of organizing and commanding it, were intrusted to Henry O'Donel, Count del Abisbal. This force was composed of the *elite* of the best troops; and the chiefs of it, or the greater number of them, detesting the tyranny under which they groaned, resolved to exterminate it for ever from the Spanish soil. Collected on one point, animated by the same sentiments, bound to each other by the same interests, they lost no time in concerting the means of striking a decisive blow; the plan was definitively arranged, the requisite communications established, and all their measures taken. The Commander-in-chief could not possibly be ignorant of what was passing around him, and with this certainty in the minds of the associated officers, they conceived the project of bringing him over to their views, giving him the direction of the enterprise, and investing him with the command of the liberating army.

He heard their overtures with pleasure, and promised every thing that was required of him: but
this man, who was no stranger in the bye-ways of
treachery, and who has since raised his perfidy to
the very acme, by a trait of cowardice that will for
ever couple his name with contempt, instead of
seconding the movements of the patriots, who had
unfortunately deemed him worthy of their frater-
nity, disconcerted the plan, and imprisoned Quiroga, Rotten, O'Daly, Arco Aguero, and San Miguel;
men who would have immortalized themselves, had
the success of their plan been complete.

Riego was attached to the etat-major of the
Count del Abisbal, and in that situation was enabled to discover the twofold intention of his general, and the crime he was about to perpetrate. He
gave information of it to the leaders of the enterprise, warned them of their danger, and bitterly
deplored the extraordinary combination of unfortunate events that lost to Spain the happiness of
being free.

The yellow-fever now shewed itself in Cadiz, in
the army, and in the squadron destined to tran-

sport that army to the other hemisphere. This malady occasioned a postponement of the expedition, and care was taken to divide the corps forming it, and disperse them in various parts of Andalusia. Riego quitted the general staff, and repaired to his post as Captain in the regiment of Asturias, cantoned, after the last distribution, at a little village called Las Cabeças de San Juan.

The love of liberty, far from being extinct in the hearts of those who had just lost, by one unexpected reverse, the fruits of so much labour and so many sacrifices, acquired fresh strength and energy; so that far from renouncing the project which had been defeated by the treachery of the Count del Abisbal, the contrivers of it were resolved to recommence their designs, and to remove as quickly as possible the check they had sustained. The chiefs were imprisoned, some in fortresses, others in villages; they kept up a correspondence with each other, through the means of trusty agents, and more particularly with Quiroga, who, as senior colonel, was to take the command, in case of events affording a favourable opportunity for re-

newing their operations.   Quiroga was confined in
the convent of Vittoria, near Port St. Mary, and
guarded by the battalion of Arragon ; this regiment
received orders to encamp for some days on a retired spot called Las Correderas, and afterward to
march to the village of Alcala de los Garules. By
this coincidence of circumstances, Las Correderas
became the rendezvous of those who were to take
a part in the new drama ; there they renewed their
former oaths, swore to each other a fidelity incapable of being shaken, and agreed upon the detail
of operations, which could not be deferred without
compromising the welfare of their country. Quiroga was conducted by his escort to Alcala de los
Garules, and then some zealous patriots of Cadiz
engaged to concert the movement with Riego, who
was at Las Cabeças de San Juan, with the battalion
of Asturias, which he commanded as senior captain,
during the absence of his superior officers. He
received the communication with enthusiasm, and
promised to acquit himself with courage in whatever station might be assigned to him : thencefor-

ward his whole attention was devoted to secure success in the arduous undertaking.

After a series of journeys, precautions, and correspondences, it was decided by unanimous assent, that a simultaneous advance should take place on the 1st of January, 1820; Quiroga, at the head of the two regiments, de España and de la Corona, was to march on the Isle of Leon, there to wait instructions from the patriots of Cadiz, for taking possession of the town; while Riego with the regiments of Asturias and Seville, should make himself master of the head-quarters of the expeditionary army, and its commander-in-chief the Count de Calderon, and thence proceed to join his comrades.

The decisive moment arrived: at daybreak on the 1st of January, Riego assembled the corps immediately under his command, and after addressing it in a short, but energetic harangue, proclaimed the Constitution of the Spanish monarchy, as decreed by the extraordinary Cortes at Cadiz in 1812, amidst the acclamations of his troops, and the inhabitants of the village, who were not less attached to the new order of things now to be re-established, than to the person of Riego, whose character and virtues they had reason to appreciate and admire.

The morning of this eventful day was occupied by installing the Constitutional authorities, and in taking such other precautions as his position required; at night-fall he quitted the village at the head of his troop, determined to share in the dangers of his chief; but either from the rain which fell in torrents, painfully retarding his progress, or from having trusted to inexpert guides, he was unable to reach Arcos, where Calderon's head-quarters were fixed, before dawn of the following day. In this laborious march he was greatly mortified at not meeting with the battalion of Seville, that was quartered at Villa Martin, and which should have joined him several hours before; his situation now became critical and perilous in the extreme; having in front a force doubly greater than his own, cut off from his coadjutors, ignorant of their fate, and of that of the corps which ought to have acted with him. With these menacing dangers before their eyes, the courage of his soldiers began to waver;

not a moment was to be lost; the crisis was arrived, and every thing to be hazarded; an energetic and decisive measure was to be adopted, or the
fruits of so many honourable and hazardous labours
would be exposed to irretrievable loss. In this
exigency, Riego went alone, to reconnoitre the
position of the town, and returning immediately,
ordered the drums to beat to arms, gave his
officers instructions for securing the head-quarters, and entered the place with coolness and
courage. Having stationed one division of his
regiment at the entrance of it, and another in the
market-place, the seizure of Calderon and his staff
was effected with the utmost celerity. The general's guard fired upon the troops as they advanced,
but by the time Riego reached the spot to ascertain
the cause of the firing, the affair was decided, and
the prisoners were in the hands of his soldiers; the
Constitution was forthwith proclaimed, and the new
authorities were nominated and installed in their
several offices. An express, detailing these events,
was immediately sent to Quiroga, who had by this
time taken command of the troops quartered at

Alcala, but from having in his front rivers much swelled by incessant rain, over which no practicable passage could be found, he was unable to execute the concerted movement, and therefore forced to wait for a favourable opportunity.

Riego was busily employed in providing, for the security of his prisoners, with every attention to their personal comforts that circumstances permitted, and in convincing the troops quartered at Arcos of his real intentions; in so doing he encountered many difficulties, in consequence of the precautionary measures that had been adopted by the Count de Calderon.

At a short distance from Arcos is the little village of Bornos, where a regiment was stationed; of this corps the officers secretly favoured the revolution, in spite of the hostile and persecuting spirit of their colonel. Riego, well knowing the importance of bringing these troops over to his party, marched to that place with a detachment of 300 men. At the entrance of the village he halted his troop, and proceeded unattended towards the houses, where he met with some of the officers, whose sentiments he was aware were friendly to his views. He communicated to them the events of the preceding night; their patriotic feelings were roused, and the enthusiasm of liberty quickly spread through the whole battalion. The regiment was immediately put under arms, and marched towards Arcos, leaving the colonel at the head of a few convalescents just recovered from the yellow fever. Success in this second instance inspired him with fresh courage, and elevated his hopes to the highest pitch; he flattered himself with the expectation of being able to bring the whole army to aid his attempt, and as his cause was just, his intentions pure, he relied upon the special favour of Providence in behalf of an enterprise, having for its object the happiness of a nation deserving a better fate.

Being received at Arcos as brothers and friends with every demonstration of joy, Riego availed himself of these moments of popular feeling, to repeat in the most glowing terms, in presence of his military followers, as well as of the public authorities of the place, his perfect devotion, and inviolable fidelity to the Constitution that had been then sworn to.

As no intelligence whatever of the situation of Quiroga had been received, he felt the most serious apprehensions; and this uncertainty caused him the greatest perplexity; because, had any unforeseen event prevented his illustrious chief from realising his expectations of gaining the Isle of Leon, as previously calculated upon, the measures necessary to be taken with his own force, was a problem of difficult solution. To proceed to the Isla, without a certainty of its being occupied by Quiroga, would have been highly imprudent; to remain inactive, surrounded as he was by hostile troops, utterly impossible. In this embarrassing conjuncture he assembled a council of the officers under his command, who resolved unanimously, that should the expected information not arrive, the four battalions, constituting the entire strength of this little army, should march on Medina, and endeavour to gain over the military quartered thereabouts, with whom communications were already opened, and whence a reconnoissance of the commander-in-chief's position might easily be effected, Medina being only a short distance from Alcala. This interval of suspense was employed in explaining to the soldiers the nature of the enterprise, in rousing their patriotic feelings, and in convincing them how important were the advantages the nation would derive from the institutions it was about to receive, as better suited to men endowed with reasoning faculties, than the absurd and barbarous despotism to which they had been subjected.

The time agreed upon to wait for Quiroga's despatches being expired, it was expedient to put the troops in motion, but the impossibility of directing them upon Medina, was soon discovered; for the River Majaaceite, which crossed their route, was so much increased by the rains as to be impassable; and on the other hand, as their combinations demanded the utmost celerity in executing their movements, the least delay might produce the most disastrous consequences, and for ever frustrate a plan which, up to that moment, encouraged sanguine hopes of brilliant success.

Under circumstances so critical, none but men

who have seen themselves surrounded by variety of danger, can easily appreciate the desperate situation of Riego. Every other route than that to Medina, removed him from the only point upon which he could rely for support, and led him into a district, where perhaps he might be surrounded and vanquished by superior forces. Fortunately, the magnanimity that has so repeatedly shone conspicuously during his short career, aided him on this occasion; and he formed the resolution of marching to Xeres, a town between Cadiz and Seville, where, at all events, he would have means of cutting off the communication between these important points; but he had scarcely quitted Arcos, when he received the long-desired despatches, in which Quiroga detailed his transactions, and ordered him to form a junction with all possible speed.

We may now take a cursory review of the operations performed by the other division of the liberating army, not less entitled to admiration, than that which had declared itself at Las Cabeças de San Juan.

Quiroga began to move at the same time as

Riego; he had escaped from his confinement, and placed himself at the head of the detachment that had been his guard, and which was entirely devoted to him. The miserable state of the roads, and the extraordinary rise of the rivers, that blocked his passage in every direction, debarred him from pursuing the route marked out for his expedition. When the waters had subsided a little, he commenced his march, and reached the neighbourhood of Medina in the night of the 2d; the major part of the troops quartered in that town were friendly to the revolt; but deeming it advisable to reconnoitre the posture of affairs personally, he advanced to the town without an escort, and at the entrance of it met with an officer, who was in the secret, but who, from cowardly and ignoble motives, told him that the whole plan had been discovered, and that if he wished to avoid falling a victim to the fury of the soldiers, his only means of escape were in falling back with the greatest rapidity to his former position. This delusive report could not shake his steady bravery, he disdained retreat, and sending an officer to seize the general of brigade, Ano, who commanded in that quarter, beat the generale, and entered Medina at the head of his division. The troops in quarters hastily flew to arms, and formed in the public square; where they soon afterward augmented Quiroga's ranks, acknowledged him as their general, and evinced a firm determination of sharing his perils and his glories. Foreseeing the obstacles that delay might throw in his way, he forthwith put his little column in march, to reach the Isle of Leon as speedily as possible. Soon after leaving Medina, he obtained intelligence that a body of cavalry had formed the design of attacking him; to defeat this attempt, he threw out a detachment to cover his rear-guard, and the officer commanding it, favoured by the darkness of the night, succeeded so well in intimidating the assailants, that they immediately retreated at full gallop. After a night of incessant rain, and extraordinary fatigue, he found himself at daylight on the main road to Madrid, and not far from the Isle of Leon. Quiroga halted a little before he reached a small military post called Portasgo, which was attacked, and gallantly carried by the brave Lieutenant

Badenas, and thirty-six men ; the same party, almost directly afterward, succeeded in forcing the bridge of Suazo, that connects the Isle of Leon with the continent. Quiroga immediately occupied this important post, and took possession of the town called La Isla, or San Fernando.

Posterity will bestow a lasting tribute of admiration upon the chief that effected this brilliant coup-de-main, and upon those who took part in it, when history shall have recorded, that his whole disposable force amounted to no more than 900 men, for the most part destitute of clothing and equipments, all of them recruits, or very young in the service, and that the sum total of effective arms, was no more than sixty-seven muskets ! By such a force, feeble in every thing but courage and ability, was Spain restored to that independence, which, by the faults of other men, she has enjoyed so short a time.

La Isla de Leon is a rich and populous town, then held by a military force, more than the double of that commanded by Quiroga ; and it became necessary, without loss of time, to neutralize the powers of resistance these elements were capable of offering. He therefore secured the persons of the minister of marine, Cisneros, who happened to be at La Isla superintending the preparations for the expedition; of M. Antron, Colonel of the regiment of Morena, and some other superior officers; his troops were, at the same time, quartered in the two barracks, where the soldiers of the town were lodged. The latter did not oppose him in the slightest degree, and their arms were immediately delivered to the patriots. The disarmed troops were permitted to return to their homes, and the necessary subsistence for their journeys granted to them; 700 men accepted these terms, and peaceably quitted the place. Quiroga was now forced to remain inactive until he could receive despatches from Riego, and instructions from the patriots in Cadiz, who had engaged to raise the town and proclaim the Constitution. These promises were not accomplished. A division sent out to reconnoitre the road leading to Cadiz, was repulsed by a fire of musketry from the garrison of the Corta-dura, a strong fort stretching quite across the

Isthmus of the Isle of Leon, a circumstance that condemned him, much against his will, to suspend his operations for a time.

Riego, meanwhile, continued his march to Xeres, where he arrived at daybreak on the 5th, and met with an enthusiastic reception from the people;* the principal inhabitants of the place assembled at the town-hall, he was introduced to them, and greeted as the saviour of the country. Orders were given for proclaiming the Constitution, and electing the authorities to govern in its name; proceedings that took place forthwith. Riego communicated by the telegraph to Quiroga the

* Similar demonstrations of joy took place nearly throughout Spain; the nation received the change of regime with satisfaction and unanimity; and it is a calumny to say, although it has been so frequently averred, that the country was not ripe for a revolt. The general enthusiasm did indeed give way, when it was governed by men without talents, who instead of acting in support of the liberators, became their most cruel persecutors. In that unfortunate country nothing was done to make the interests of the revolution take deep root in the minds of the people, and this explains the cause of the recent catastrophe, in which liberty was destroyed by an effort, that would have been impotent, had the national arm been raised in its defence.

news of his arrival; and in reply, received intelligence of the occupation of the Isla. On the same night he reached Port St. Mary, the inhabitants of which bestowed, both upon him and his troops, the most unequivocal marks of their cordiality and admiration. At this place many of the officers who had been arrested at Cadiz, after the affair of the 8th July, escaped and joined the column; among them was the illustrious Arco Aguero, who, a few months afterward, was snatched from his friends, and the service of his country, by a premature death.

Riego's division should have reached the Isla on the night of the 6th, it arrived there, in fact, but at a much later hour than had been calculated upon, owing to the badness of the weather making it necessary to halt at Puerto Real, a little town midway between it and Port St. Mary. A junction of the two corps was at length effected amidst transports of joy and enthusiastic patriotism, heightened by the cheering expectation of speedily beholding the rest of the army, and the whole nation, rallying around the banners of liberty. After this memorable union, a general muster of the whole active force engaged in the arduous undertaking, took place, and it was found not to exceed 3,000 men ; we particularly solicit the attention of our readers to this circumstance, because it has been generally believed throughout Europe, from exaggerated statements given in the public journals of all parties, that the Constitutional army was in sufficient strength to resist the attacks of that which still remained in submission to the despotism of Ferdinand. We shall quickly have reasons to be satisfied it was not numerical force, but the liberal spirit, the courage of the patriots, and the simultaneous co-operation of all the provinces, by which this handful of heroes was preserved from destruction and death. The page of history does not record a revolution threatened at its birth by so many dangers and untoward accidents, achieved by a force so diminutive.

A skilful organization of this force, from its smallness, became the more necessary; Quiroga was confirmed in his rank as commander-in-chief, Riego appointed his second, and Arco Aguero, an

officer, who, to an unconquerable bravery united
the most consummate knowledge of military tactics,
nominated chief of the Etat Major. The army
was divided into two corps, one under the immediate orders of Quiroga, and the other under those
of Riego; a junta of government was formed from
those men, not of the military profession, who had
taken a leading part in bringing about the new
order of things. A manifesto was issued, representing to the nation, in calm and dispassionate language, the evils it was intended to remove, and the
benefits that would result from a judicious administration, founded on reason and justice; Quiroga also addressed to the King a letter, couched
in terms of firmness and respect, the arguments of
which could be opposed only by brute force, the
last resource of tyranny and oppression. The population of the Isla received their illustrious deli-
verers in the most flattering manner; the Constitution of 1812 was solemnly proclaimed, the new
authorities nominated and acknowledged, and
every one waited with the impatience of anxious
expectation for the declaration of Cadiz, as it was

considered this important town ought to give the watch-word of liberty to every other in the monarchy.

The progress of events did not, however, keep pace with the eager desires of the patriots. General Campana, who commanded in Cadiz, and afterward cast an indelible stain upon his reputation by the horrible massacre of the 10th of March, had adopted the most tyrannical measures, to prevent a demonstration of the feelings that agitated every heart ; on the other hand, Joseph O'Donnell, brother of Count del Abisbal, commanding the military district of Algeciras, placed himself at the head of some regiments, and was in full march against the Isle of Leon. General Freire had succeeded the Count de Calderon, and collected the expeditionary troops, of which several corps had promised to declare for the Constitution, at the same time as those under Quiroga and Riego, but either from want of opportunity, or inclination, had not redeemed their pledge. The clergy, with the Bishop of Cadiz at its head, intrigued in every possible way, spreading the contagion of fanaticism

and seduction in all directions; on all sides obstacles accumulated, and unfavourable symptoms
every where appeared, but these difficulties neither
discouraged the army, nor damped the zeal that
animated its chiefs.

The 10th day however brought with it additional
buoyancy to their hopes; the regiment of the
Canaries saluted the Constitutional colours, and
were received with open arms; this example was
followed by a brigade of artillery, under the command of Lopez Baños. Riego, with 100 picked
men, made a sortie from the island to cover the
entry of these troops, and succeeded in taking some
prisoners from the royalist army, that had pushed
its advanced posts nearly to the bridge of Suazo.
His next exploit was to check the movement that
O'Donnel was making upon Medina, which he effected with great bravery and skill. It was now
resolved to attack the Carraccas, a vast and important arsenal of the marine, separated from the
island by a narrow arm of the sea: this enterprise
was intrusted to 400 men under the command of
Garcia, and crowned with complete success. The

garrison, consisting of 500 men, voluntarily joined the Constitutional Army, which obtained by this capture a vast depôt of arms, ammunition, and other military stores. This victory led to the design of an assault upon the Cortadura, which waited only for the return of Riego, who was to lead one of the columns destined to execute the *coup-de-main.* Several circumstances, however, delayed the attempt, and in the interim this officer was disabled for several days from the effects of a very severe fall. As soon as he recovered his health, he was detached with a respectable force to Port St. Mary, then occupied by a division of the royalist cavalry, but which fell back at the approach of the patriots. On his arrival at that place, he had the mortification to receive information, that a scheme concerted by Colonel Rotalde for opening the gates of Cadiz to the liberating army had totally failed: this disappointment rendered a retrograde movement to the Isla a measure of necessity, notwithstanding the friendly reception he again experienced from the inhabitants.

The dangers that now menaced the patriot's

army, presented themselves in a much more formidable attitude than they had been expected to assume. Freire was approaching with a force ten times greater than that which they could oppose to him : all the routes were occupied by the enemy ; all their means of co-operation frustrated ; and not one favourable chance cheered this devoted band of brave men, closely penned up in a corner of the Peninsula. Every plan of operations they devised, was thwarted by perils imminent, astounding, and various, whilst inaction would be incalculably more fatal ; means of evading total ruin appeared impracticable ; and every day passed in this alarming apathy augmented their difficulties, and threatened to accelerate the catastrophe. In this situation of perplexity and dismay, Riego conceived the project of hazarding every thing, to win the cause by one daring exploit ; and to make a sortie from the Isla with a detachment of troops, for the purpose of trying this chance of gaining an accession of strength, or opening the way for more extensive co-operations. His design was not warmly applauded by the other chiefs; in fact, it presented but little probability of success, from not being founded on the basis of prudential calculations; but the soldiers of his division eagerly seconded the wishes of their leader, and supported him with the most positive demonstrations of readiness to sacrifice their lives, or achieve the glorious enterprise. The fear of creating discord at a moment so critical, operated in favour of a measure that cool reflection, or tactical caution, would not have sanctioned, and the sortie was finally decided upon.

On the 27th Riego sallied from the Isle of Leon at the head of 500 men, picked out for this hazardous and extraordinary expedition; they traversed Chiclana and Conil, and reached Vejer, where he halted for a few hours to publish the Constitution, and nominate new authorities. He then advanced to Algeciras, an opulent and populous town, where he flattered himself with being able to procure some assistance from Gibraltar, but therein his expectations were disappointed: however, the inhabitants of Algeciras received his troops in the most friendly manner, and furnished him with some supplies he was in want of. At this place he issued a proclamation, setting forth, in terms of appropriate energy, the advantage Spain would derive from a unanimous adoption of the Constitution. At Algeciras was composed the celebrated military song called " Riego's Hymn," one of the many brilliant and spirited productions that, by their sentiment and melody, have so frequently roused the Spanish soldier to a pitch of enthusiasm, the fervour of which can be duly appreciated by many a brave hero of the British soil. During his stay there, he received an order from Quiroga strictly enjoining his immediate return to the Isla; a recall as momentous as it was unexpected, but founded upon the most imperative motives. Quiroga well knowing that the column was closely followed by a very superior force under Joseph O'Donnell, feared that it might be cut off, besides his own situation was very far from being secure, as the remainder of the expeditionary army was advancing upon it in all directions, and in a state of preparation that portended serious disaster to him. Under these circumstances, and with no more troops than were absolutely necessary to man the fortifications round the town, this detachment of 500 men would be an inestimable reinforcement. Riego did not hesitate a moment to put his column in motion, on its counter march: on reaching the environs of Vejer he fell in with a corps of the enemy's cavalry, in considerable force, which appeared determined to obstruct his route; on seeing this body prepared for action, and although he had not a single horseman at his disposal, he made a disposition for attacking it, and advanced with the unanimous cry of *Viva la Patria.* The steady countenance of these brave men disconcerted the satellites of tyranny; the cavalry retired without attempting any offensive operation, and left the column a free passage. On arriving at Vejer, Riego ascertained that all the roads leading to the Isla were occupied by the enemy, and that it would not be possible for him to force a passage with so small a number of men, without exposing them as a sacrifice to their own bravery. Nevertheless he did not renounce the determination of obeying his orders, nor was he discouraged by the numerous obstacles that thwarted his design; he passed the night at Vejer, where a patriotic banquet and a ball were prepared for himself and his intrepid followers by the inhabitants. He also obtained there some stores that were indispensable; and after many fruitless efforts to fulfil the directions of his commander-in-chief, he ultimately resolved to change his plan of operations, and formed a design, worthy of his enterprising spirit, that, to say the least of it, flattered him with the possibility of a fortunate issue. He lost not a moment in executing this measure, which was to direct his march towards Malaga: in this route O'Donnell's troops constantly hung upon his rear, and repeatedly attacked him, but he as invariably obtained decisive advantages over his assailants, and reached his destination on the 18th.

Riego's reception at Malaga was less flattering than what he had experienced in other places; his troops were attacked in the streets, and the inhabitants rendered him no assistance. Being one of the principal sea-ports of the Mediterranean, a place of great wealth, and the residence of many public functionaries, it is not very surprising that the fear of compromising their commercial interests should have repressed the ebullition of patriotism. Well aware of the dangers that would gather round him were he to remain long within its walls, he hastily withdrew from it, and took the road to Antequerra.

This expedition, from its commencement, gave unequivocal indications of the fate that awaited it: his first object had failed, because, contrary to his well-grounded hopes, the people did rise *en masse* to support the cause, doubtless, from knowing that his column was part of the military force which had begun the revolution, they conceived it to be in possession of the necessary means for bringing the same to a fortunate termination. On the other hand, the hostile cavalry, assuming courage from the retrograde movements of the Constitutionalists, harassed them incessantly, and prevented the smallest respite to their fatigues. Notwithstanding these difficulties, in spite of the certainty that they could obtain no assistance, no reinforcement, and that there was no point of support they could direct their march upon, the courage of the soldiers was not weakened; they pursued their route steadily, fought with intrepidity, and under the pressure of privations unusually severe, and perils more than commonly disheartening, they cheered each others' spirits by singing the favourite hymn and patriotic songs. From Antequerra he proceeded to Ronda, where he found an enemy's force more than twice the strength of his own ; this he attacked and succeeded in dislodging, and afterward obtained a supply of rations from the town. At Puertollano, after an interval of a very few days, another series of attacks began, and was scarcely discontinued for an hour, until he arrived at Montilla, in which he made a short halt, and during that repose, his mind was employed in tracing the plan for ulterior operations. At some leagues from Montilla, the immense chain of mountains called the Sierra Morena offered a secure asylum, but it could not be gained without taking a very circuitous route, nor without passing through Cordova, capital of the province, and the seat of a rich and powerful aristocracy. The attempt was daring beyond the limits of common valour; but they resolved to risk every thing, and, if necessary, stake their lives upon the justice of their cause.

On approaching Cordova, they discovered a body of troops advantageously posted to dispute their entrance into the city ; the column, that by losses in the preceding skirmishes, was now reduced to 330 men, beat and dispersed this body, and marched into the city ; other royalist troops that were in garrison there, remained in the barracks, and took no part in the affair. Riego's troop passed triumphantly through the streets, singing the patriotic hymn with a spirit and animation that formed an inexplicable contrast with the nudity and want, of which every man presented the most unequivocal marks. It would be difficult to depict the scene in that city ; a little band of soldiers, exhausted with fatigue, almost famished, covered with the dust and dirt of long and toilsome marches, surrounded and followed by an immense population, mute with astonishment and admiration ; the balconies of the houses were filled with spectators, who only broke the general silence by exclamations of enthusiasm ; the public authorities remained passive, the clergy was stupified ; after a few hours of rest, this devoted column quitted Cordova, and pursued its route towards the mountains.

On the 11th of January it reached Bienvenida, after a fatiguing march, but there the perils that invested it on every side, appeared insurmountable; and the chances of success, or escape in a body, so far beyond the limit of military computation, as to induce a determination to disband, and endeavour individually, with all the precautions their safety demanded, to rejoin their brothers in arms, shut up in the Isle of Leon.

The conduct of the soldiers forming this expedition, furnished, during the short duration of it, a fine example of courage, discipline and generosity; they had undoubtedly rendered themselves, by their general conduct, worthy of a better fate; but the irresistible force of circumstances is so far above the power of human efforts, that the fire of genius is stifled, the noblest intentions frustrated, and the most heroic sacrifices rendered abortive, by its overwhelming weight.

In this memorable, but short, campaign, public spirit was roused in other parts of the Peninsula, and at all points an active co-operation with the liberating army began to shew itself. Riego reached the Isla of Leon in safety, and shortly after Quiroga's army was saluted by the whole of Spain, as the instrument that Providence had made use of to deliver the kingdom from the execrable evils that preyed on its vitals.

The Constitutional system was every where proclaimed, accepted by the King, and put in action all over the country with perfect unanimity. The electoral assemblies were convoked in obedience to the new code, and General Quiroga was returned as Deputy for Gallicia, his native country. Being now under the necessity of resigning the command of the army, he determined to place it in the hands of Riego, notwithstanding his being junior to many of the other chiefs then serving under his orders. This important trust was gratefully accepted by him, and without the least delay, he organised a numerous and effective corps, sufficient to keep in check the machinations of the enemies of liberty, both internal and external. His labours in an undertaking so arduous, were favoured with results consonant to his wishes ; and in September 1820, he went to Madrid, whither he was called by the voice of public gratitude, and an anxious desire of seeing the brave and highly-gifted individual who had taken so extraordinary and active part in the deliverance of his country.

His entrance into the capital was a triumph; an immense multitude waited for him outside the gates, and on his arrival took the horses from his carriage; the air resounded with shouts of welcome; joy and enthusiasm enlivened every countenance; it was indeed the civic festival of patriotism and gratitude. The king, Ferdinand! received the hero of Las Cabeças in the most gracious manner; children overwhelmed him with caresses; the public bodies were prodigal of their homage and admiration; personages of the most exalted stations declared themselves honoured by ranking him among their friends; and in no instance has there been shewn testimonies of esteem and respect, apparently more sincere than those thus lavished upon Riego. He received these proofs of attachment from his fellow-countrymen, with a modesty that placed his character in the most advantageous point of view.

But this victory gained over the passions of servilism, awakened the jealousy of a knot of men who then ruled the destinies of Spain, was the precursor of a scheme of persecution, almost without parallel in the records of history, which the base contrivers pursued until their hatred was sated with the blood of their unfortunate victim. The ministers pretended to see in these ebullitions of general satisfaction, the most alarming symptoms of discord and rebellion; they insinuated that public tranquillity was endangered by Riego and his friends; songs, hymns and rejoicings were proscribed as the incipient devices of conspirators; they did more; they carried their perfidy to the extent of circulating a report, which unhappily found believers, that his design was to establish a republic; and threw out hints, that any act of revenge, however atrocious, might be sanctioned against a man, whose object was to overthrow an established form of government, and trample the fundamental laws of the realm under his feet.

The Marquis de las Amarillas, then at the head of the war department, concealed his criminal intentions under the mask of hypocrisy; he has

since displayed himself as an unprincipled con-
spirator against the Constitution; and it is now
well known, that from the beginning of the persecution of Riego, down to the present time, there
has not been a single measure adopted by him,
which did not directly tend to abolish the Constitutional regime. This man, in whom the other
ministers, and the deputies to the Cortes, blindly
placed their confidence, ordered the army in the
Isle of Leon to be disbanded. A measure of this
nature, for which no one could assign a reasonable
motive, alarmed all true patriots, and caused
general dissatisfaction. In Madrid there were two
patriotic clubs, but until that order, the speakers
had confined themselves, in their harangues, to explaining the articles of the Constitution to the
people; but when this odious decree against the
army was promulgated, the clubs resounded with
cries of indignation, and taunts of bitter invective
against the ministers. The latter resolved upon
a mode of action, that even under an arbitrary government, would have been most unwise and dangerous; they shut up the clubs, and surrounded

the houses in which they were held with an armed force ; the orators were thrown into prison ; the streets of the capital filled with artillery ; proclamations and ordonnances every where posted up, in order to make the people believe the country was on the very brink of a dreadful abyss, and that Riego's was the only guilty hand which had dragged it there. The ministers made a report of these proceedings to the legislative body ; their discourses were pompous and artful commentaries upon the iniquitous and illegal steps they had taken. M. Arguelles distinguished himself on this occasion by emphatic phrases, a mysterious, unnecessary reticence, and alarming predictions. Many members who sided with the ministry improved upon these specimens of quaint oratory. M. Martinez de la Rosa declared, that the best means of defending the liberty of the people, would be derived from supporting the government; and described the fêtes given to Riego, in which no instance of popular excess occurred, as scandalous orgies, forerunners of a civil war, and of all the disasters that could afflict a polished nation. On the following day a virtual sentence of exile was pronounced against Riego, who was destined to vegetate in one of the provinces.

The ministerial journal, conducted by one of those unblushing sycophants, always ready to prostitute their pens to him who pays them best, and who are familiar with calumny or treason, when it suits their base purposes, represented the conduct of Riego in the most odious colours, and the unjust procedure that had been adopted against him, as the only method of restoring social order, and consolidating the Constitutional system.

Language is inadequate to place in its true light the falsehood, injustice, the want of gratitude, of which the ministers, and the deputies who supported them, were guilty of; their case was so weak, so bad, that they were unable to adduce a single well proved fact against the victim of their malice. What was the utmost they could say? Why, that their self-love had received a wound, and that they were afraid the power they had made themselves masters of would escape from their feeble grasp. Such horrible conduct on their parts, produced an abundant harvest of misery. By the dissolution of the army in the Isla, the only well organised military body then on foot in Spain, they encouraged faction, and left without protection or support the very system they had made the stepping-stone to their own aggrandisement. By calumniating Riego and his friends, they drew a defensive bulwark around the props of servilism. By proscribing patriotic societies, they extinguished public spirit; in fact, by proclaiming a false and mistaken moderation, they proffered this perfidious deceit to those who were able to make use of it, and who actually did use it afterward to undermine the foundations of liberty.

They shewed themselves, at the same time, to be very inexpert political calculators, for Riego was become popular, and his popularity was decidedly beneficial to the new order of things; whereas they, so far from being held in estimation by the people, could only muster a few adherents, all of aristocratic principles, consequently enemies of the people, and of the general welfare. The serviles and conspirators exulted in these proceedings, which were far beyond the compass of their most sanguine hopes; the door, thenceforward, stood wide open to them; the signal had been given, they took advantage of the crisis, and the epoch of Riego's persecution, was the commencement of that vast chain of machinations, those hydra-headed conspiracies, of that tissue of crimes, which have terminated in the establishment of absolute power, and the letting loose of all the scourges that now ravage unhappy Spain.

Examined in its connexion with foreign politics, the persecution of Riego may be considered as a signal, given to the cabinets of the allied powers, for commencing their operations in conjunction with the internal conspirators. The revolution in the Isla, and the amazing progress it made in a short time, at first petrified the crowned despots with astonishment; but no sooner were the promoters of that unexpected event, exposed to the persecutions of those men who falsely professed to be firm friends of the Constitution, and to have an interest paramount to every other in preserving it, than the latter were regarded as powerful and useful auxiliaries. A decisive resolution was then taken to overthrow a political order which menaced the gothic edifice of privileges and arbitrary power; and an implicit confidence was placed in these imprudent, or rather vicious, men, who placed deadly weapons in the hands of those who eagerly sought an opportunity for using them.

The author of the present memoir was an ocular witness of the anxieties shewn by the diplomatic agents of foreign powers at the Court of Madrid. At first, it was feared the Spanish ministers did not possess sufficient nerve to execute the resolutions they had taken; they were encouraged by deceitful eulogiums, excited by adroit flatteries; and when, by these means, they were spurred into the contest, and persuaded to maintain it, these worthy agents, the ready tools of their no less worthy employers, exulted in their victory, and the roads were incontinently covered with extraordinary couriers, bearing to Louis, to Francis, and to Alexander, the unexpected tidings of an event that paved the way to a certain triumph.

Riego endured his exile with heroic resignation,

and passed several months in his native province of Asturias, to which he had been ordered. During his seclusion, the ministry found it necessary to make some reparation for the injuries they had heaped upon him, because the public indignation loudly censured them for ingratitude and baseness, and he was in consequence appointed Captain General of Arragon.

In this post he displayed great activity in the public service, condescendence and kindness to the soldiers, and did every thing in his power to infuse into the military body an attachment to the cause of the Constitution. Unassuming, assiduous and indefatigable in business, benevolent and popular, he was the pride of the army of Arragon, the admiration of the inhabitants of Saragossa, and other cities within the province. Arragon would not have been the hot-bed of conspiracies, and the head-quarters of faction, as it afterward became, had the successors of Riego, in this important command, followed his example, and displayed zeal and activity even in an inferior degree.

During his sojourn in the Asturias, he gained

such an ascendancy in the esteem of his countrymen, so entirely convinced them of the sincerity
of sentiment, the uprightness of intention by which
he was actuated, that at the period for electing deputies to the Cortes, they readily delegated their
powers to him; he was therefore chosen deputy
for the Asturias, and as such, under the necessity
of leaving Saragossa. This was a severe blow to
the political opinions of the province, and to those
of the inhabitants who were heartily attached to
the Constitution; they foresaw he would be succeeded by men inclining more to power than to
liberty, more disposed to advance their personal
interests, than to promote their country's welfare.
Riego was a constant attendant in the patriotic
society, he ascended the tribune to inculcate the
love of liberty, and spread it among the people;
he carefully watched the proceedings of its enemies,
and frustrated them with no less ability than courage. He brought over to his opinions many persons whose inveterate prejudices made them contemplate institutions, grounded upon the immutable
laws of reason and justice, as dangerous and dread-

ful innovations; in fact he shewed himself not merely as a chief, but an apostle preaching the doctrine of liberal ideas; and it will be difficult to find a man imbued with similar sentiments, and gifted with so much energy and zeal to disseminate them.

Before going to Madrid, he went into Catalonia and Valencia; this was a journey of congratulation, in which he received testimonies of respect not less brilliant than those his presence had before elicited in the capital; and he adroitly turned these proofs of public esteem to the advantage of the noble cause to which he had consecrated his life. In his progress he laboured incessantly to strengthen the Constitution; he encouraged the public authorities, formed intimate connexions with men who had shewn a decided character as patriots, he harangued the people, and electrified the youthful portion of it; he repressed the hopes of the factious, and frequently witnessed tears of gratitude, cries of enthusiasm, and marks of regard, that his presence excited wherever he stopped. The political chief of a province through which he passed, when writing to

the ministers, used these remarkable expressions:
" The public feeling in this district has totally
changed since it has been visited by General
Riego ; we have now no conspirators. Every one
loves the Constitution ; children read it at school ;
the priests explain it from the pulpit, patriotic
hymns are sung in every company, fêtes are given
to the people, societies are formed, service in the
militia is eagerly sought, enmities are reconciled,
suspicious persons disappear ; in fine, the arrival of
General Riego has acted, like the regenerating
principle, upon a province that shewed alarming
symptoms of being guided by a very bad spirit."

Riego arrived at Madrid, and soon entered upon
the duties that had been assigned to him; these
were of a very delicate nature, as the preceding
legislature had not accomplished the wishes, nor
fulfilled the expectations of their constituents;
much was therefore required for giving stability to
the Constitutional government, and promoting
public happiness. The true patriots had to enter
the lists against the party that had usurped the
ministry, and under the mask of moderation, con-

cealed the most sinister views and dangerous intentions. From his renown, his zeal, and unwearied activity, the opinion of such a man as Riego was of great weight in the contest of parties; a circumstance that imposed upon him the most cautious circumspection, and exacted the most discriminating tact. Generous in debate, but yet incapable of yielding to arguments that were incompatible with the good of the people, he placed himself in the ranks of those deputies who were actuated by principles similar to his own; and his vote was always given in favour of the most liberal and decisive measures. He spoke but little, and only on important occasions; then his harangues were dignified by the noble simplicity of a patriotic soldier, without disguising the sentiments by which he was animated, without that species of concession and insincere complaisance now unfortunately so common in representative bodies; he did not confine himself to explaining his own views of a question, he successfully combatted those of others, and carried conviction to the minds of such members as were misled by prejudices inimical to the public good.

During a month he occupied the president's chair, and displayed from it qualities that he was not supposed to be endowed with ; it was feared the natural impetuosity of his character would make him lose sight of the nice equilibrium, the firmness of mind, the impartiality that so important and delicate an office requires. As president, he retained the opponent parties within the bounds of moderation, and checked the sallies of imprudent zeal, ill-will, or exasperation. Riego was one of those who foresaw the consequences of foreign plots against the Constitution, and exerted himself with no less perseverance than address, to engage the depositaries of power in frustrating such treacherous wiles, and adopting measures of vigour highly expedient under circumstances so critical. But the fate of Spain was sealed; for men, with the word moderation in their mouths, and wilful patricide in their hearts, had opened a free passage to a torrent that nothing could resist.

The events of the first week in July, proved the predictions of Riego and those who acted with him, to be founded on a correct knowledge of the men and measures opposed to them; the capital was invested by the rebel guard, the patriots fled to arms, and Riego was not one of the last; he refused taking a command, and preferred fighting in the ranks with his countrymen, and dying, if such might be his lot, upon the altar of his country. The ardour excited among the troops by his presence, gave great uneasiness to the traitor Morillo, who was then plotting to destroy the Constitutional system. Riego shewed his accustomed moderation, and exhibited convincing proofs of his unaffected character; in common with all other patriots, he celebrated the triumph of the good cause, but he plainly perceived the imprudence of giving themselves up to a dangerous inactivity. On this memorable occasion, his friends frequently heard him say—" We have begun the strife; our enemies will return to the charge; we must neglect nothing; let us be on our guard; a blind confidence may destroy us; we must labour indefatigably."

The invasion of Spain took place. The French army assembled at the foot of the Pyrenees, under pretext of forming the " Cordon sanitaire," penetrated into the Peninsula. The Cortes passed a decree for removing the royal family and themselves, from Madrid to Seville, and thence to Cadiz. In the latter part of this journey, Riego would not lose sight of the King, who, he was well convinced, sought an opportunity of throwing himself into the arms of the enemy. On reaching Cadiz a single *coup-d'œil* was sufficient to shew him the dangerous predicament in which the friends of liberty were placed; and he perceived the moment was arrived for making the greatest sacrifices, for striking the last blow, and for completing every preparation to meet the impending storm that was now ready to burst over them.

He now formed the design of making a sortie from Cadiz, with a column of 1000 men; his object was to shew himself in the provinces he had formerly traversed with so much success in making proselytes; and, if possible, to augment the means of defence, enrol volunteers, rouse the energies of the people, and organise a system of popular resistance similar to that which, a few years before, had baffled the designs, and repelled the efforts of the greatest conqueror of modern times.

Every man then at Cadiz, who was well affected towards his country, highly approved of this noble and generous project ; they publicly declared that this step alone would collect an immense mass of resistance, and repress the audacity of the invaders: they knew how powerful is the influence of *name* in political convulsions ; how irresistible the magic of an exalted and well earned reputation.

By a fatality closely interwoven with the series of misfortunes by which Spain was at last subjugated, this plan could not be put in execution; want of money was the pretext assigned for refusing him permission to serve his country by achieving another brilliant exploit.

A very short time proved the magnitude of the fault that had been committed. The progress of the enemy was rapid, the broken spirit of the troops, the indifference of the people, afforded him a bloodless triumph. Treasons, purchased by the corrupting gold of the Holy Alliance, multiplied with frightful celerity. At last, General Ballesteros who, by his anterior conduct, had placed the steadiness of his principles beyond a doubt, and who, at the head of an army of 20,000 men, enthusiastically devoted to the cause of freedom, guarded the almost impenetrable defiles that separate Andalusia from Castile, signed a dishonourable capitulation, and gave up that important province, the only resource of the Constitutionalists. The French now advanced without striking a blow, and Cadiz was invested both by sea and land.

In this mortifying situation of affairs, the error just alluded to pressed upon men's minds in all its gigantic enormity; and Riego was once more called forth to delay the coming ruin. He was destined to take command of a corps at Malaga, under the orders of General Zayas, and he repaired thither with the utmost expedition, fired by the hope of checking the torrent of disaster, and averting some of the evils arising from the previous want of exertion. The means confided to his discretion were not, however, of a nature to inspire him with much confidence, and even these were not available from the excessive scarcity of money. He convoked the municipal body, and required it to procure him the sums that were absolutely necessary for enabling him to commence offensive operations; he forbore to issue peremptory orders on this subject, and left to the legitimate authorities the care of raising funds, knowing that these authorities, being better acquainted than himself with the resources of the surrounding country, and the private fortunes of individuals, would apportion the contribution with equality and justice.

This circumstance has been greatly distorted to the eyes of the world by calumny and misrepresentations, the usual weapons of tyrants and their abettors. The *London Courier* in particular, was pleased to give a long detail of the vexations and depredations ordered or sanctioned by a man who, through the whole course of his career, both military and political, invariably gave proofs of a most inoffensive character, and of the noblest sentiments. This accusation was put forth by the ministerial writer after Riego's death, an incident that augments the atrocity of the charge, and shews what portion of honourable feeling the author of it can lay claim to. We may be permitted to remark *en passant*, that this odious species of tactic has been resorted to only by one party ; by that which labours to establish thrones upon no better foundation than the wreck of the people's happiness; to cheat the laws into silence, and make them crouch to the caprices of absolute power, and immolate the human race to the corruption of courts, and the intrigues of venal cabinets. Such conduct, may worthily stand in comparison with that of the populace of Madrid on the 2nd of November, 1823, when the bodies of the *liberals*, the half-consumed remnants of mortality, were torn from the hallowed sanctuary of the grave, to glut the savage vengeance of a frantic mob; but the man who can turn from the voice of reason, or the call of justice, and listen to the wild howlings of a faction thirsting for blood, will extenuate any excess however infamous. Letters are now lying before us, from respectable merchants at Malaga, contradicting in terms the most positive, these lying recitals, and representing the conduct of Riego during his stay at that place, as guided by scrupulous impartiality, greatness of mind, and moderation.

Malaga being surrounded by numerous French corps, Riego was forced to evacuate it, and hs situation became critical in the extreme; to whatever point he directed his march, he was beset by dangers. He plainly saw the public spirit was broken; lost that courage which, until now, was wrought to the highest pitch by his presence, and with which he would have performed prodigies, had not his labours been overthrown by impotent or treacherous counsels. He took a route towards the mountains of Grenada, pursued by superior forces that kept him almost incessantly skirmishing. On approaching Loja, he found French troops posted in the neighbourhood, and being forced to change his direction, determined to join the army of Ballesteros, which was then in a state of shameful inactivity from having signed a scandalous capitulation, although his corps was composed of excellent soldiers, strongly attached to the cause, who reviled, with bitter execrations, the treachery of their general.

Near Priego, he came in sight of the first troops of this army, posted in a defensive attitude, and in much greater force than his own division. At this appearance of hostility, the Constitutionalists were greatly discouraged; Riego felt a noble confidence in himself, and was never deserted by hope; he halted his column and advanced alone; at the head of the opposing force, he found the battalion of Asturias, the very regiment that had supported him in proclaiming the Constitution at Las Cabeças' He addressed himself to these men, who still retained a respectful and affectionate remembrance of their former commander; his first words subdued them; they ran to him with shouts of *Viva la Constitution;* the remainder of the column followed this example; after embracing his old comrades, he placed himself at their head, and began his march to the head-quarters of Ballesteros.

This officer was petrified at beholding him, the very appearance of Riego was the bitterest reproof that he could receive for his detestable conduct; the latter accosted him with frankness and good will, explained to him the present posture of affairs, and proved that a favourable opportunity now offered of striking a decisive blow, that would be fatal to the French forces in Andalusia; dwelt with animation upon the immortal glory he would acquire by seizing it, conjured him to place himself at the head of both divisions, and even offered to give up his own command, and serve him in the capacity of aid-de-camp; he avoided every thing like reproach or recrimination; he sued to him in the language of friendship, but in vain. Ballesteros was inflexible; he thought himself bound to observe a perfidious capitulation—he who had broken the most sacred oaths—he who had violated the most solemn promises—was determined to drain the cup of infamy to the very dregs.

During this interview, the other generals of Ballesteros' army, accomplices in his treason, collected some troops, among whom they distributed money, and began to form them in line, fronting Riego's division, which remained at the entrance of the village. Apprized of this danger, and seeing that all farther efforts would be of no avail, he returned to his companions in arms, and commenced a retreat with every untoward chance against him. He took the direction of Jaen, and in the neighbourhood of that city, encountered a body of French troops; but having fortunately occupied some

heights, and shewing a determination to defend his
ground to the last extremity, the enemy did not
attempt to molest him. Farther retreat was still
necessary, and then, assailed in every direction,
worn down with hunger and fatigue, having to make
rapid marches through roads cut up and destroyed
by the rain that fell in torrents ; the courage of his
soldiers began to sink under such accumulated dis-
tresses, and desertion, to an alarming extent, took
place. At every halt he discovered a serious dimi-
nution in the number of his men. He was harassed
by continual skirmishes, and fatigue had increased
beyond farther endurance ; not one consoling hope
presented itself to these brave fellows, who had displayed so much courage and energy. In this appal-
ling dilemma they reached Jodar, where all the
officers were of opinion, the only remaining measure to be adopted, was to disband, and each one
seek his safety as he best could. This was done,
Riego's aids-de-camp conjured him to escape with
them to the coast, and embark for Gibraltar ; but
still desirous of serving his country, still confiding
in the justice of the cause to which he was devoted,

he declared that he would still buffet the torrent of calamities that ingulfed him, and resolved to traverse the country in disguise, and join the intrepid Mina in Catalonia.

That the heroism of such a resolution may be duly appreciated, it will be necessary to describe the state Spain was in at that time. The troops of France had traversed it in every direction, without encountering the slightest resistance; the treason of the generals, had depressed the courage of the soldiers; the provinces were in a state of apathy, from the very stupor of fear; to which may be added, that to reach Catalonia, it would be necessary for him to travel over nearly one half of the Spanish territory, occupied by foreign troops, or bands of the factious; the royalist authorities kept on foot a police severely vigilant, and Riego was every where known; in fact, nothing but the intervention of extraordinary good fortune, could preserve him from the imminent perils that surrounded him.

All these opposing difficulties were pointed out by his friends, but even the entreaties of friendship could not shake his firm resolve ; and accompanied by two faithful individuals, who were determined to share his fate, and sacrifice themselves with him, he quitted the army, and placed himself under the protection of Providence. After a journey of a few leagues, he entered a little village in the Sierra Morena to obtain some refreshment, where being recognised, he was seized and delivered up to the royalists.

Willingly would we spare our readers the contemplation of a frightful picture, which, as faithful historians, we are bound to place before them. The history of human nature, in the extremity of its perverseness, can hardly furnish an example of baseness, cruelty, and barbarism, parallel to that which it is our duty to describe. The fate of General Riego is notorious, or the reader would suppose we are speaking of a savage nation, wandering in the deserts, and degraded by every crime that leaves a stain upon the character of man.

The capture of such a man as Riego, was a frantic triumph for that party, which, by the aid of French bayonets, had broken down the Constitutional edifice, and now sought to take immeasurable vengeance, mounted on an ass, and escorted by brigands, who vied with each other in maltreating and insulting him; he was conducted to Madrid. At every village he passed through, the rabble was called together to see the captive hero, and revile him as a ferocious beast of prey, which the hunters were leading to the slaughter. At Madrid he was confined in a barrack, and given in charge to the Count de Torre Alta, one of the captains of the rebel guard that attacked the capital on the night of the 6th July, 1822. This traitor to his country, whose name would not be handed down to posterity, but for the maledictions of every feeling and generous man, exhausted upon his victim all the cruelties that his polluted mind could devise; he immediately thrust him into a filthy dungeon, with no other furniture or convenience, than a couple of planks; for twenty-four hours he received no food, and the only means allowed for allaying his thirst, was from a dirty and disgusting bucket filled with water. He posted at the door of the dungeon, some of the most daring wretches of the populace, to upbraid and abuse his prisoner with horrible ferocity; these outrages he bore with the equanimity of a noble character. A soldier placed as sentinel over him, one day said, " Were you not in prison, I would murder you." " Were I not a prisoner," replied Riego, " you would not dare to look me in the face."

As the form of a trial was necessary, to give even a semblance of legality to the sacrifice that was previously determined should be made; the cause was brought before a blood-thirsty tribunal called La Sala de Alcades, a court that had been dissolved by the Constitution; but the Regency established by the Duke of Angouleme had restored it, and found it the ready instrument of their vengeance. Riego was a general, commissioned by the king, and as such could be legally tried by a court-martial only. But men who had in contemplation a violation of the laws of justice and humanity, would not wait for the formation of the proper tribunal. The accusers were for some time at a loss how to designate the crime of their prisoner; and it was at last resolved to try him in his quality of deputy to the Cortes, for having voted in favour of the King's removal into Andalusia.

Never has there been a more atrocious abuse of delegated power; never has there been seen a more impious mockery of the sacred functions of tribunals. As the Regency did not recognise the legality of the Cortes, how could one of its courts take cognizance of the proceedings of the Cortes? or what law forbade the deputies to vote the expediency of a journey for the monarch? What code provides a punishment for such an act? What right had been thereby infringed; what part had been violated by prescribing that journey? The minds of men are bewildered in reflecting upon the iniquity of so unhallowed a process. Civilized Europe has already shewn its abhorrence of this act incomparably base.

The accusation itself was a monstrous tissue of vague reproaches and low-bred insults: the whole of the trial was characteristic of the spirit which dictated the horrible contrivance. As no advocate of Madrid would take upon himself to defend the accused, it was therefore necessary to assign him counsel officially, and he was permitted to say only a few words in behalf of his client; for when he began to plead, the populace that had filled the court, demanded with savage cries the heads of Riego and his defender. In consequence of this tumult, the doors were closed, and a hasty termination put to the scandalous scene.

Sentence of death was pronounced and put in execution with unheard-of rigour : by the Constitutional code the punishment of the gibbet had been abolished, but this was the mode by which Riego was destined to suffer. The sentence was communicated to him three days before the time appointed for his execution : he was then confined in a chapel, and constantly surrounded by ignorant fanatic monks, who imbittered his last moments by their bigoted and barbarous zeal. At last, on the 6th November, Riego was taken to the scaffold on a hurdle drawn by an ass, and died without betraying the slightest symptom of fear, unsteadiness, or regret.

Thus terminated the life of a man whose name has resounded throughout Europe, accompanied with benedictions from the true friends of liberty : thus died Riego, the hero of Las Cabeças, one of the saviours of his country ; an innocent victim, who laboured for the good of his fellow-countrymen, and spread numberless benefits among them : thus fell the man who could have destroyed with a breath the throne of his persecutor ; and yet had the generosity to believe that even the soul of a despot was susceptible of humane sentiments. It will be unnecessary to engrave upon his tomb, " Exoriare aliquis nostris ex ossibus ultor." He will have avengers without this incitement ; his enemies are preparing for him this posthumous triumph, and which may possibly be a signal for the emancipation of the human race.

THE END.

Printed by J. F. Dovz, St. John's Square.

www.ingramcontent.com/pod-product-compliance
Lightning Source LLC
Chambersburg PA
CBHW061038050726
47592CB00004B/1502